Larry Bird

By
Matthew Newman

Edited By
Dr. Howard Schroeder
Professor in Reading and Language Arts
Dept. of Elementary Education
Mankato State University

Produced & Designed By

Baker Street Productions, Ltd.

CRESTWOOD HOUSE

Mankato, Minnesota
U.S.A.

LIBRARY OF CONGRESS CATALOGING-IN-PUBLICATION DATA

Newman, Matthew.
Larry Bird.

(SCU-2)
SUMMARY: A biography of Larry Bird, basketball player for the Boston Celtics and winner of two consecutive Most Valuable Player awards, the only non-center to have accomplished this feat.
1. Bird, Larry, 1956-   — Juvenile literature. 2. Basketball players — United States — Biography — Juvenile literature. (1. Bird, Larry, 1956-   . 2. Basketball players.) I. Schroeder, Howard. II. Title. III. Series: Sports Close-ups.
GV884.B57N48   1986   796.32'3'0924   (B)   (92)   86-16524
ISBN 0-89686-314-X

International Standard Book Number:	Library of Congress Catalog Card Number:
0-89686-314-X	86-16524

PHOTO CREDITS

Cover: Noren Trotman/Sports Chrome
Richard Mackson/Sports Illustrated: 4
AP/Wide World Photos: 7
Sports Chrome: 8, 29, 41
UPI/Bettmann News Photos: 11, 20, 38-39, 47

Carl Skalak/Sports Illustrated: 13
Rick Clarkson/Sports Illustrated: 15, 16, 19
Focus on Sports: 23, 26, 33, 34, 37, 42
Jerry Wachter: 24-25
Manny Millan/Sports Illustrated: 30-31

Hwy. 66 South Box 3427
Mankato, MN 56002-3427

TABLE
OF
CONTENTS

In the beginning: The Playground Days 5

Growing Up in French Lick 6

Springs Valley High School 8

The Bird That Wouldn't Fly 10

Bird Finds A Nest:
Indiana State University 12

Larry Leads the Sycamores 14

The Almost-Perfect Season 17

The NCAA Championship Game 17

The Highest-Paid Rookie Ever 20

Rookie of the Year 21

The NBA Championship 22

The NBA's Most-Complete Player 32

The 1982-83 Season 35

Magic Versus Bird:
The Second Time Around 36

Larry Bird: Mr. Clutch 43

The 1985-86 Season 44

Off the Court: The Hick from French Lick . . . 46

Larry Bird's Professional Statistics 48

Many people think that Larry Bird is the best basketball player to ever play the game.

4

IN THE BEGINNING:
THE PLAYGROUND DAYS

The three brothers always left the house early in the morning. Mark, Mike, and the younger one, Larry, all took turns dribbling and passing the ball to one another on their way to old Hubbard's court in the Deerfield Subdivision. When they got to the court, one of the older brothers would usually take the first shot. It would be well into the evening before the last shot was taken.

On almost any given day, the Bird brothers could be found on the court shooting "hoops." They played endless games of two-on-one and "Horse." They made up their own game called "Showtime" in which each brother practiced his favorite trick shots. They often pretended to be famous basketball players as they copied their heroes' moves on the court.

"I never wanted to leave the court until I got things exactly correct," Larry remembers. "Even as a kid in grade school, my wish was to become a pro."

As soon as he was old enough to walk, Mark and Mike taught Larry how to shoot a basketball. Later, at school, Larry practiced by tossing wadded paper in a wastepaper basket. At home, he cut the bottom out of an old coffee can and shot a rubber ball through the "basket" over and over.

"It's funny," Larry says. "I used to go watch my older brother, Mark, play when he was in high school. Everybody was cheering for him. I wanted to be that guy. I wanted the people cheering for me."

GROWING UP
IN FRENCH LICK

Larry Joe Bird was born on December 6, 1956. He grew up in French Lick, a small resort town located in the southern hills of Indiana. Like most kids in the neighborhood, Larry loved playing basketball. It was, and still is, the most popular sport in Indiana. Almost every boy dreams about being a professional basketball player. Very few children are able to hold onto this dream. Larry is one of the few who did.

"Basketball is my whole life, and it will always be my whole life," Larry says.

The Bird family lived in a small house. All six children slept in two bedrooms. Joe Bird, Larry's father, worked as a wood finisher in a piano store. Georgia Bird, Larry's mother, worked long hours in many of the restaurants and factories around French Lick.

"My kids were made fun of for the way they dressed," Mrs. Bird remembers. "Neighbor kids had their own basketballs or bikes. My kids had to share a basketball. A friend of Larry's would say, 'If you can outrun me down to the post office, you can ride my bike for ten minutes.' Larry used to run his tail end off."

When he was about four, Larry got his first basketball on Christmas day. But the ball didn't last too long. "My ball was one of those cheap rubber balls. I was so proud of it that I stayed up for hours bouncing it. I left it by the stove that night, and when I got up the next morning it

Larry had to work hard to learn to play basketball. He still works hard.

6

had a big knot in it. My parents got me another ball, and I remember Mike, Mark, and I wore that one completely out."

Even as a child, Larry Bird knew the value of effort. As a basketball player, he didn't have great natural skills. There were others who could run faster and jump higher. "I remember we used to practice in the gym in high school," Larry says. "Then on the way home, we'd stop and play on the playgrounds until eight o'clock. I played when I was cold and my body was aching and I was so tired . . . I don't know why, I just kept playing and playing."

SPRINGS VALLEY
HIGH SCHOOL

As a teenager, Larry never stopped thinking about ways he could improve his game. Each time he stepped on the court, he found a new lesson to learn. But he knew the value of his lessons off the court, too.

"In school the only thing I thought about was basketball," he says. "But I went to class and did my homework. I felt sorry for the players who didn't, and I tried to talk to them. I knew they were going to have a tough life."

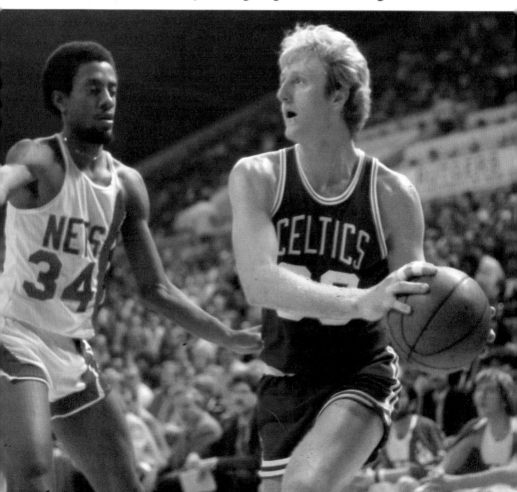

At seventeen, Larry was the star player on the Springs Valley High School basketball team in French Lick. But when he first joined the team, Larry wasn't even the best player.

"I never saw a kid who played basketball so much," Larry's high school coach says about Bird. "He didn't have a car or much money, so he spent his time at basketball."

By the time he was a junior, Larry had grown to 6'4" in height. But he only weighed about 160 pounds. His teammates called him "Matchstick." Larry began to lift weights and develop muscle. As a senior, he was much stronger and weighed 200 pounds. He had also grown to 6'7".

Larry's playing improved quickly, and he became one of the best players in the whole state. Still, Larry had one problem — he passed the ball too often. One day, his coach said Larry would have to turn in his uniform at half time if he didn't start shooting more.

From then on, Larry started to take more shots. As the coach thought it would, this helped the team win more games. In time, Larry would hold nearly every scoring record at Springs Valley. In his senior year, he averaged 30 points and 20 rebounds a game.

After the season, Larry made the Indiana All-Star team. Some were surprised to see a player from such a small school given this honor. For Larry, however, the success story was only just beginning.

Larry still looks for ways to improve his game every time he plays.

THE BIRD
THAT WOULDN'T FLY

More than two hundred coaches wanted Larry to attend their colleges. They knew that with Bird in the lineup, their basketball programs had a good chance of winning.

There was one school in Florida which sent Bird an airline ticket. Larry packed some clothes and went to the Indianapolis airport. He had never been on a plane before. When he saw a jet take off for the first time, it scared him. He turned around and went home.

In the fall of 1974, Larry enrolled at the University of Indiana. This school was only about an hour from his home. When he got there, however, Larry felt very strange. There were thirty thousand students in the school. There were only two thousand people in all of French Lick. "The university was so big," Larry said. "And I didn't know anybody. I had no one to talk to."

After only twenty-four days, Larry got homesick and left school. He decided to go to a much smaller school, the Northwood Institute in West Baden, Indiana. This school only had about 160 students.

Again, however, Larry had trouble living away from home. There weren't many good players on the basketball team. After three weeks, Larry quit and went home again.

Back in French Lick, Larry wondered if he would ever find the right college. He spent time at the playground, where he worked on his game. He also got a job driving a garbage truck.

In 1974, Larry couldn't find a college he was comfortable with.

"It was the best job I ever had," Larry said later. "I told the guys, 'I'm going to go to college to get a little education. Then I'll come back and be the boss of you guys.'"

At the time, however, even Larry didn't know where he was headed. His father had just passed away. Larry, his mother, and his grandmother all had to work to pay the bills. In that same year, Larry got married, but a divorce soon followed.

"I'm a lot smarter on the basketball court than I am in life," Larry admits.

BIRD FINDS A NEST: INDIANA STATE UNIVERSITY

All during this period, Georgia Bird worried about her son. The people around town were saying that Larry was a quitter.

One day, a man named Bill Hodges came to Mrs. Bird's door. Hodges told Mrs. Bird that he was a basketball coach at Indiana State University in Terre Haute. Mrs. Bird did not greet him warmly.

"Why are you bothering him?" Mrs. Bird asked. "He doesn't want to go to school. Leave him alone."

But Mr. Hodges would not be turned away easily. He drove around French Lick until he spotted the tall blond teenager coming out of a laundromat with his grandmother.

Larry has always been a small-town person. Coach Hodges was the first to tell him how famous he could become.

"We went to the grandmother's house and talked for an hour," Hodges said later. "Even though he didn't agree to come to Indiana State right away, I felt sure then that he would."

At first, Larry turned down Hodges' offer of a scholarship to go to Indiana State. It wasn't until the coach spoke of a player Larry used to play against in high school that Larry changed his mind. "I remember him," Larry said. "He could have been a great college player."

"They'll say that about you some day," Hodges replied. "That you could have been a great college player."

For the first time, Larry saw what staying out of college might mean. "That hit a nerve in him," Hodges said. "That made him decide to come to Indiana State."

Once he had made up his mind, Larry went one step further. He had never been one to boast. Still, he made Coach Hodges a promise: "Indiana State may not be very good right now," he said, "but it will be when I get there."

Because Larry was a transfer student, he had to sit out his first season at Indiana State. "That was one of the best things that ever happened to me," Larry says. "My game matured a lot. I worked on my passing, my dribbling — my overall game. I was ready to play my sophomore year."

LARRY LEADS THE SYCAMORES

Larry's first league game with the Indiana State Sycamores took place in November of 1976. The Sycamores —

Larry did a great deal to help the Indiana Sycamores become a winning team.

14

who were 13-12 without Larry — won their first game by twenty-one points. Bird had 31 points and 18 rebounds.

Larry led the Sycamores to a season record of 25-2. This was Indiana State's best record in history. Bird averaged 32.8 points a game.

By the time Larry was a junior, the word about "The Bird" was spreading all across America. Over 250,000 fans turned out to watch the Sycamores play. Indiana State finished the season at 23-9. Larry averaged 30 points and 11 rebounds a game.

One thing Bird didn't enjoy was talking to reporters.

Larry was nicknamed the "Silent Sycamore," for his silence with reporters.

He was still very shy. The press nicknamed him the "Silent Sycamore."

"The reporters were coming in after games, and the only one they wanted to talk to was me," Larry explained. "Some of my teammates didn't mind, but others did. I knew we were heading for trouble. We had a good team and I didn't want to do anything to mess up our season. So I decided if I didn't talk, the reporters would have to talk to the others."

After the season, the Boston Celtics named Bird as their number one draft choice. This was unusual, because pro teams rarely draft a college player until after his senior year. But the Celtics wanted Bird badly. They hoped Larry might turn pro early, and give up his senior year.

To the delight of the Sycamore fans, Bird decided to finish college. "I wanted my college degree," Larry said.

THE ALMOST-PERFECT SEASON

In 1977, the Sycamores again started the season fast. They won eighteen games in a row. Before each home game, fans waited in the arena aisles. When Bird came out to warm up, they went wild with cheers. A new record called "Indiana Has a New State Bird" came out on the radio.

Meanwhile, Bird began piling up records of another sort. In the final game of the regular season, Larry had 49 points and 19 rebounds. This was the most points ever scored by an Indiana State player in a single game.

THE NCAA CHAMPIONSHIP GAME

By the finals of the NCAA tournament, the Sycamores winning streak reached 33-0. They became only the eighth team in history to reach the NCAA title game undefeated.

Only one team — Michigan State University — stood in the way of the national college crown. The Spartans were led by a talented guard named "Magic" Johnson.

Everyone looked forward to the Bird-Johnson match-up. Both players were top rated. But each had a different style. Magic was fast and flashy. Bird was quiet and not nearly as slick. Both players, however, were known as winners.

"To me, it's a very serious game," Larry said, comparing himself to Johnson. "I can't be laughing like he does out there. I just hope when it's over he ain't laughing at me."

The two teams tipped off in Salt Lake City, Utah before a national television audience. At the time, it was the largest TV audience ever for a college game.

Right away, the Spartans showed their game plan — keep the ball away from Bird. Two or three men were around Bird at all times. Larry's teammates couldn't get the ball to him very often. And when the Sycamores fell behind by sixteen points, it was too late for a comeback. Bird was held to only nineteen points, his lowest total in five NCAA play-off games.

Michigan State's 75-69 win dashed Bird's dream of a national title. In the end, the Sycamores finished with a 33-1 record.

Even in defeat, Larry had much to be proud about. He was named the NCAA Tournament's Most Valuable

Despite Larry's best efforts, the Sycamores lost to Michigan State in the NCAA finals.

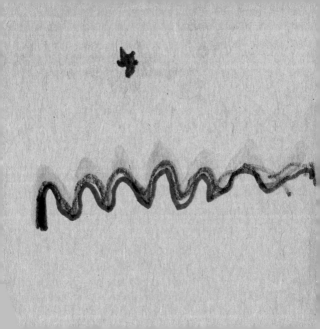

Player. He was also voted a Unanimous All-American, and the Associated Press' and United Press International's Player of the Year.

THE HIGHEST-PAID ROOKIE EVER

Larry had served some big goals by staying on at Indiana State for his senior year. He had earned a degree in physical education. He had taken the Sycamores to the edge of a national title. And, he had increased his value as a professional basketball player to the Boston Celtics.

"If the Celtics want me, they'll call," Larry told his agent. "If they don't want me, they won't call . . . I'm goin' fishin'."

Larry was sure that the Celtics would call. Once the best team in the National Basketball Association, the Celtics had since become one of the worst. The Celtics' record the year before (29-53) was their worst in almost thirty years.

After a while, the Celtics and Bird agreed to a contract.

On June 6, 1979, Larry signed a five-year pact worth $3,250,000.00 (US). At the time, this made Larry the highest paid rookie in the history of sports.

Unlike the promise Larry made before playing at Indiana State, he gave the Celtics a cautious warning about the impact he would have. "Very few people can turn a team around by themselves," Bird said, "and I'm not one of them."

By mid-season of his rookie year, Bird was rated by NBA coaches as one of the top defensive players in the league. The Celtics were winning again. Many said Bird's play — on offense and defense — was the key difference.

"Larry works so hard, he makes me look lazy," Celtics' center Dave Cowens said.

"When you combine his defense, his passing, and his scoring, you have to say that he can become the greatest all-around forward ever to play this game," the Celtics assistant coach, K. C. Jones, said.

One man who was very pleased with Bird's team-play was the Celtics' president, Red Auerbach.

"The ultimate beauty of the kid is that he'll do anything — absolutely anything — to win, even if it means giving up personal statistics," Auerbach said.

ROOKIE OF THE YEAR

In his very first pro season, Bird led the Celtics to a stunning turn around. The Celtics' regular season record was 61-21. They won more than twice as many games than

Larry Bird became the highest paid rookie in basketball history, when he signed with the Celtics', Red Auerbach.

they had the year before. The Celtics won the Atlantic Conference Championship. They went all the way to the Eastern Conference Division Finals before bowing out to Philadelphia, 4-1.

Around the league, players and coaches began to see that Bird was much more than a great shooter. He was a fine passer and rebounder as well.

Larry averaged 21.3 points, 10.4 rebounds, and 4.5 assists a game for the season. He was named as a first string NBA All-Star. He also made the All-NBA and All-Rookie teams. He placed third in the vote for the NBA's Most Valuable Player. And, he beat out his long-time rival, Magic Johnson, for the Rookie of the Year honors.

"I probably would have paid them to let me play," Larry said happily after getting the award.

THE NBA CHAMPIONSHIP

"This is the same atmosphere I knew in college," Bird said. "Everybody is always kidding everyone else. I love it! It's really important, too, because it keeps the team loose."

By the middle of the 1980-81 season, the Celtics were about as loose as a team can get. They had won twenty-five out of their last twenty-six games. Bird was averaging 28 points, 15 rebounds, and 7 assists a game.

"Sometimes it's scary," Bird says. "When I'm at my best, I can do just about anything I want, and no one can stop me. I feel like I'm in total control of everything."

22

Larry helped the Celtics become winners.

Larry and his Celtic teammates are introduced to the crowd.

Larry loves to shoot long-range "bombs" from all over the court!

During this stretch, Bird would often toss up long-range "bombs" and turn away before the ball even reached the basket. "I already know it's all net," he said.

The Celtics ended the regular season at 62-20. They then met the Chicago Bulls in the first round of play-offs. The Bulls had won fifteen of their last seventeen games. But, the Celtics cooled them off by taking four straight games.

The Celtics then moved on to meet the Philadelphia 76ers. Right away, the 76ers took a 3-1 series lead. But somehow, the Celtics came clawing back. Down by six points with less than two minutes to play, the Celtics rallied to win Game Five. The Celtics then came from seventeen points down to win Game Six.

In the seventh and deciding game, the Celtics again fell behind early. Late in the fourth quarter, they still trailed the 76ers by six points. At this point, Bird took control of the game.

In a matter of seconds, Bird made two key steals, two free throws, and a big rebound. To top it off, Bird also scored the winning basket. The final score was 91-90.

"I wanted the ball in my hands for that last shot," Bird said later. "Not in anybody else's hands in the world."

In the NBA Championship Series, Boston faced the Houston Rockets. The Rockets knew that they would have to hold Bird in check if they hoped to win.

"I'm going to cover him so close I'll tell you what kind of cologne he's wearing," one Rocket boasted. "I'm going to be able to count the hairs on his neck. He'll be seeing my number in his sleep."

As it turned out, the Rockets did keep Bird from scoring a lot of points. Still, Bird made an impact. In Game One, Bird made what Red Auerbach has called "the greatest play I've ever seen."

After missing from eighteen feet away, Bird hustled after the rebound. He caught the ball in mid-air at an angle behind the board. Still airborne, Bird switched the ball from his right to his left hand. As he put up his shot, Bird crashed beyond the base line. Only the roar of twenty thousand Boston fans told him the shot had gone in. Sparked by Larry's effort, the Celtics came from behind to win the game.

After five games, the Celtics led the series 3-2. In Game Six, Bird halted a Rocket comeback by calmly scoring a long three-pointer near the end of the game.

"I didn't even know it was a three-pointer," Bird says. "I caught the ball in shooting position; nobody was around, and I just released it. Heck, when I'm open for a shot I usually feel like I *can't* miss it. And when I have a shot like that to get us a game, I've got to take it. Because I know I have an excellent chance of making it."

In this case, Bird's shot not only won the game — it won Boston the NBA title. The final score was 102-91. It was the Celtics' fourteenth NBA crown, and Bird's first.

In only two seasons, Bird had taken the Celtics to the top of the NBA ladder.

*Bird had taken the Celtics to the NBA finals in only
two seasons.*

"Larry Bird," Coach Fitch said, "made us winners
because he is the complete basketball player."

Larry joins Danny Ainge on the bench during a game.

THE NBA'S MOST-COMPLETE PLAYER

"If I wanted to break records, I wouldn't be the all-around player that I am," Larry Bird said after the 1981-82 season. "How many championships you've won . . . how many games you've won . . . those are the important things. Individual records don't excite me."

Whenever Bird has played, he has always taken on the role needed — as shooter, passer, or rebounder — to help the team win. Whether it means taking the clutch shot or diving for a loose ball, Larry always puts the team first.

"Maybe some players don't care if they win all the time," Bird says, "but I do. I hate losing!"

"The one thing you have to avoid when you talk about Bird is his statistics," Red Auerbach says. "It's his presence, the total way he commands attention on the court that counts."

"The things he can do are just unbelievable," Magic Johnson says. "He beats everyone because he plays such a smart game."

Larry's "court sense" did not come along by accident. He is known as one of the hardest workers in the NBA. He worked so he could dribble and shoot with both hands. He developed his shooting range so he could take three-pointers and layups. He pushed himself to become a tough rebounder. He found the special knack for timing passes at just the right moment. Overall, he has prided himself on taking on new challenges at every step of his career.

*Larry prides himself on developing all kinds of
basketball skills.*

Larry is a great passer!

"I always try to know exactly what's happening on the court," Larry says. "I want to know exactly what I can and cannot do. How can I score on this guy who's guarding me? Can I drive around him? Or can I take jump shots from the foul line? I decide what I think is going to work. Then I go out and try to do it."

In the 1981-82 All-Star game, Larry was voted the Most Valuable Player award. Leading the Eastern Conference to victory, Larry had 19 points, 12 rebounds, and 5 assists.

The Celtics finished the 1981-82 season with a record of 63-19. They again met the Philadelphia 76ers in the Eastern Conference finals. This time, the 76ers won the series.

After the season, Bird made the first All-NBA team. He also finished second in the league's Most Valuable Player voting to Moses Malone.

THE 1982-83 SEASON

In the 1982-83 season, the Celtics did not go as far as they had in 1981-82. Still, Bird gave Celtic fans some special thrills during the year.

In February and March, the Celtics were in the middle of a slump. On March 29th, the Celtics reached the bottom. The lowly Indiana Pacers beat the Celtics by twenty-nine points in Larry's home state.

The Pacers and Celtics faced off again in the Boston Garden on March 30th. This time, Bird made sure the outcome was different. At half time, Larry already had twenty-four points.

With the Celtics' fans screaming, "Larr-ee, Larr-ee!" Bird added twenty-four more points in the third quarter alone. This set a new record for the most points ever scored by a Celtic player in one period.

By the end of the game, Bird had fifty-three points — a Celtic record for total points in a regular season game. The final score was 142-116, Boston.

The Celtics finished the year at 56-26. In the NBA play-offs, they defeated the Atlanta Hawks 3-2 in a mini-series. In the semi-finals, however, the Celtics lost four straight to the Milwaukee Bucks.

Afterwards, Bird made a promise: "I'm gonna go back home this summer and work harder on basketball than I ever did before."

MAGIC VERSUS BIRD: THE SECOND TIME AROUND

As the Celtics opened the 1983-84 season, the memory of the team's quick exit from the play-offs the year before was still fresh in their minds. The whole team looked forward to doing much better in the season ahead.

As it turned out, Bird led the Celtics in nearly every category — on both offense and defense. His season totals of 1,908 points, 796 rebounds, and 520 assists added to his claim as the NBA's most complete player.

In the 1983-84 season, Larry was the NBA's most complete player.

Larry always wants to be the best — that includes
shooting free throws well.

38

The Celtics again met the Bucks in the post-season play-offs. This time the Celtics won, 4-1.

This set up a meeting with the Los Angeles Lakers for the NBA crown. A familiar face — Magic Johnson — was the leader on the floor for Los Angeles.

"Everybody wants it. The world wants it," Magic said about the Bird-Johnson rematch. "What makes it really something to see is that it's not like we're just two great scorers, because you can shut scorers down. We do so many other things. Even if one of us isn't scoring, we make our presence felt."

In Game One, the Lakers jumped out to a 24-9 lead. Magic led the Lakers on several breakaway baskets. Bird started out slowly. He only had five baskets as the first half ended.

In the second half, Bird began to get going. Still, the Lakers won, 115-109. While Bird and Magic were close in points scored, Boston's loss on their home court seemed to be a bad sign for Celtics fans.

The Lakers also led most of the way in Game Two. But the Celtics came back to win in overtime, 124-121. Oddly, neither Bird nor Johnson played well.

"It was a great win." Bird said, "but I hate to think how I'd feel if we had lost, after I lost the ball off my foot near the end of overtime."

In Game Three, the Lakers ran away from the Celtics and won, 137-104. After the game, Bird said the Celtics played like "sissies" for not getting back on defense.

The Celtics met the Lakers for the 1984 NBA crown.

Kareem Abdul-Jabbar (right) and Larry fight for control of the ball.

In Game Four, the Celtics played tougher. Still, they again had to go into overtime to win.

In Game Five, Bird went wild at both ends of the court. He scored 34 points and had 17 rebounds to lead the Celtics to victory. But the Lakers came back to take Game Six. This left the series tied at 3-3.

Before the largest pro-basketball television audience ever, the Lakers and Celtics tipped off Game Seven in the Boston Garden. The Celtics were able to slow down the Lakers' fastbreak. In turn, the Lakers tried to shut down Bird. But this left Bird's teammates open for easy baskets.

In the third quarter, the Celtics scored nine unanswered points. The Lakers were never a serious threat after that. "It got away from us," Laker star Kareem Abdul-Jabbar said later. "I don't think it matters who has the most talent. They had the best team."

The Celtics' 111-102 win earned them their fifteenth NBA crown. For his part, Bird averaged 27.4 points and 14 rebounds a game during the seven-game series. After the season, he was named as the NBA's Most Valuable Player.

LARRY BIRD: MR. CLUTCH

In the 1984-85 season, Bird showed why he was indeed the NBA's Most Valuable Player. When it got to crunch-time, Bird could be counted upon.

"No one has won more games in the last couple of years

than Larry Bird," says Julius Erving of the Philadelphia 76ers. "He wants the ball towards the end of games because he always thinks he's going to make the shot."

On Janaury 27, 1985, Portland led the Boston Celtics 127-126 with only seconds left in the game. Bird's teammates got him the ball. Bird sank a shot from behind the backboard to win it, 128-127.

Two nights later, Detroit led Boston 130-129 late in the fourth quarter. This time Bird weaved his way in for a lay-up to score the winning basket.

Bird finished the season with a 28.7 scoring average, which made him second in the league. He also was eighth in rebounding, with a 10.5 average.

Though the Celtics were beaten 4-2 by the Lakers in the NBA Championship Series, Bird did his part. For the second year in a row, he was named Most Valuable Player. He is the only non-center in NBA history to do this!

THE 1985-86 SEASON

Before the three-point shoot-out at the mid-season All-Star game, Bird said, "All right, who's playing for second?"

Backing up his boast, Bird sank eleven shots in a row to win the $10,000.00 (US) first prize.

All season long, Bird found new ways to amaze people. At one of the early season Celtic workouts in 1985-86, Coach K.C. Jones offered to cancel practice if anyone could sink a shot from half-court. Bird sank a basket on his very first try!

After a Christmas Day loss to the Knicks, the Celtics went on to win a record number of games in a row at the Boston Garden. At season's end, the Celtics' record of 67-15 put them ten games ahead of the second place Milwaukee Bucks.

Bird finished the regular season in the top ten in many categories. He had the best free throw, and three-point shot percentage in the league. He led all forwards in assists. He was once again among the league's best in scoring (25.8) and rebounds (10.0).

In the post-season play-offs, the Celtics lost only once while defeating Chicago and Atlanta in the early play-off rounds. The Celtics then went on to meet the Milwaukee Bucks in the next round of the play-offs. The Celtics had little trouble with the Bucks, as they swept the series, 4-0. This set up a show down between Boston and Houston for the NBA title.

The Celtics won the first game of the Championship Series by the score of 112-100. The Celtics also took the second game, 117-95. In the two games, Bird had 54 points, 16 rebounds, 20 assists, and 8 steals.

Led by Ralph Sampson's 24 points and 22 rebounds, the Rockets came back to win Game Three by the score of 106-104. In Game Four, Larry Bird broke a 101-101 tie by sinking a long three-pointer with only 2:26 left in the contest. The final score was 106-103 in favor of the Celtics.

The Rockets won Game Five by a score of 111-96. During the game, a fight broke out between 7'4" Ralph Sampson and 6'1" Boston guard Jerry Sichting. The fight seemed to breath new life into the Rockets.

In Game Six, however, the Celtics left no doubt as to which team was tougher. The Celtics led by thirty points in the third quarter. The final score was 114-97, in favor of Boston. Bird played forty-six straight minutes, and refused to come out of the game even when the outcome was no longer in doubt.

"I've never been so pumped up in my life," Bird said later. "This takes the cake. They knew my team came to play basketball."

Larry Bird was named Most Valuable Player in the Championship Series. The Celtics ended the year with an amazing 50-1 home record, easily the best in NBA history. Bird averaged 24 points, 9.7 rebounds, and 9.5 assists in the six-game series. By taking the series 4-2, Boston had earned its sixteenth NBA crown. After the season, Bird was named as the NBA's Most Valuable Player for the third year in a row.

OFF THE COURT: THE HICK FROM FRENCH LICK

"I really enjoy being Larry Bird, the basketball player," Larry says, "but the superstar stuff I don't need. I really don't need anybody to build my ego. I've already proven that a white boy who can't jump, can play in this league."

There have always been two sides to Larry Bird. On the

Larry doesn't feel any need to be known as a superstar — he just loves the game.

court, Larry shows no mercy. In the words of one player, "When you look into his eyes, you see a killer."

But there is another side. Off the court, Larry likes being just a regular guy. As he puts it, Larry is, and always will be, "a hick from French Lick."

Neither fame nor money will ever change this side of Larry Bird. He still loves wearing tee-shirts, blue jeans, and a baseball cap. In the off-season, Larry always returns to French Lick to visit friends and family.

"I've seen a lot of places, but I've still never seen any place quite as good as Indiana," Bird says. "It's my home. I feel comfortable there. People treat me just as another guy, and that's how, more than anything, I want to be treated."

After Larry won his first NBA championship, the people of French Lick paid him a big honor. They renamed one of their streets Larry Bird Boulevard. They also put up a street sign shaped like a basketball. But, Larry takes it all in stride. As he drives down the street in a pickup truck, it's hard to imagine he is perhaps the best basketball player ever. And that's just the way Larry likes it.

LARRY BIRD'S PROFESSIONAL STATISTICS

Year	Team	FG (Pct.)	Reb.	Ast.	TP (Avg.)
1979-80	Boston	693 (.474)	852	370	1745 (21.3)
1980-81	Boston	719 (.478)	895	451	1741 (21.2)
1981-82	Boston	711 (.503)	837	447	1761 (22.9)
1982-83	Boston	747 (.504)	870	458	1867 (23.6)
1983-84	Boston	758 (.492)	796	520	1908 (24.2)
1984-85	Boston	918 (.522)	842	531	2295 (28.7)
1985-86	Boston	796 (.496)	805	557	2115 (25.8)
	Totals	5342 (.509)	5897	3334	13,432 (24.7)